Scherzo Furiant

Scherzo Furiant

Poems by

Louis Gallo

Cover design by Shay Culligan

ISBN: 978-1-950462-62-9

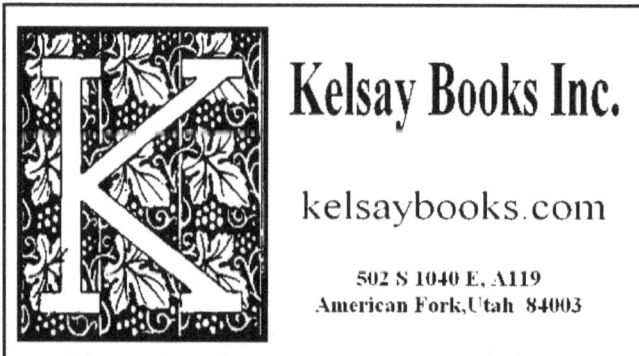

Kelsay Books Inc.

kelsaybooks.com

502 S 1040 E, A119
American Fork, Utah 84003

Acknowledgments

"Recruitment (with Bosco)," *Fictive Dream* [as prose] (British); "For the Blue Heron I Saw in South Carolina," *Belle Reve;* "Sears Nights," *Straight Forward;* "You're Beautiful," *Pretty Owl Poetry;* "Scherzo Furiant" *Pennsylvania Literary Journal;* "Once With Jen and Sue and Bob Dylan," *Poetry Quarterly;* "Fiona Came By," *Adanna Literary Review;* "Double Negative," *OffCourse Literary Journal;* "The Best Po-Boy," *Arlington Literary Journal;* "I Placed a Bone In Arkansas,"* and "In Passing," *Clinch Mountain Review;* "The Workers," *Work Literary Journal;* "Dream," *North of Oxford;* "Rereading Ulysses in Medias Res . . .," *Adelaide Literary Magazine;* "As I Stood There," *Offcourse Literary Journal;* "Sugie, When You Coming to Get that Turkey?"* and "Prayer," *Spillwords Press;* "Grasshopper While Reading Isaiah," *Pennsylvania Literary Journal;* "The Big Picture—Smelling the Roses,"* *Utopian Science Fiction Magazine.*

Contents

Brass

Percussion

Orchestra

Re-Reading Ulysses in Media Res after Many Decades while Steering "The Santa Maria" Westward into the Dying Sun

As Leopold savors his kidney with relish, his eye also cocked
on an advertisement for Plumtree's Potted Meat, and Molly
murmurs yes and Paddy Dignam returns to life, I scan
the flaming sky for traces of god and find god nowhere
and everywhere, the mechanic's monkey wrench aligning
strips of Victorian wallpaper, as Stephen converts the Paraclete
into a mythic aviator who defied Olympus, as, as . . . as
I fry a filet of catfish in Bertolli's extra virgin olive oil
with minced roasted garlic, a pinch of sea salt, sprigs
of parsley and chives, a sprinkling of capers, smoke
from the pan rising, smoging the kitchen, we two choking,
she switching on the exhaust fan because the fire burns
too bright, and Leopold's bar of lemon soap begins to speak
in Nighttown as Circe transforms us all into swine
and I turn to embrace her thirty years earlier because
she has just walked into the room, outside a snowstorm,
the cold reddening her cheeks, her eyes glittering
like warm ice, and I, chef wearing a splotched apron,
tug her forward, remove the peacoat, kiss her chapped lips,
and she, yes, we can eat later, burned fish, as Stephen
seeks succor from the Virgin, as Leopold grieves his Rudy,
Paddy's coffin sinks and . . . as everything exponentializes,
the heat heatifies, the universe expands and begins
to freeze, and Boltzmann unhangs himself from the rafters
and renounces his equations, and we consummate, yes,
nothing else matters, and Horace repeats *dulce et decorum est*
but scratches out *pro patria mori,* and information exceeds
its digital allotment, we become one and the fish is delicious

though the cat goes blind and a book drops to the floor
and Aeolus, that windbag, blows out our candle, and yes,
she says and I say yes and we know yes means no to time,
to clocks, to the centuries and eons, to Hades & Hell
and rigor mortis, deliquescence, entropy and grave wax
and Icarus falling.

Woodwinds

As I Stood There

L'éternel silence de ces espaces infinis me terrifie
—Pascal

As I stepped onto the porch to check
The rain, the weather, and leaned against
A column post as Baby slept
In the nearby rocking chair,
Configurations of air and mist
Got me dreaming as I stood there,
Fancying that we dawdled on
A globe of rock that spun around
In empty space as it sped somewhere,
Lugging with it planets and fire,
An atomic fever spilling light
Into my eyes as I stood there
Wondering about the stars and moons
And asteroids, all headed for
The edges of the universe
Billions of light years in the past.
The vertigo had reached such pitch
I lifted up my drowsy cat
And sat me down where she had slept,
Dreaming of a man no doubt
Standing there in waking sleep
Who dreams about odd marvels that
No sleepy cat would dream about.
And now with Baby on my lap
I close my eyes and drive out thought.
I yield to others who stand awake
On porches as day begins to break.

In Passing

I saw her in passing, only passing,
in the passenger seat of a car
as I stood on the porch, guessing
the rigor of wind and snow
that might still whack us another blow
in this late blooming spring, only in passing
and that for a split second or so
as her honeyed hair flared wild with the wind
sweeping into that open window,
and I, worried and thinking of weather,
fell in love with that fleeting girl.
Oh, we were never together, I knew her not
and in likelihood will never see her
again. But that is the way with weather—
absolute yet passing.

For the Blue Heron I Saw in South Carolina

Just want to say thanks
though now you're hundreds of miles away
and I'm back home . . .
for suddenly being there
in the marshes of Barefoot Landing
solitary, dignified, beautiful.
I shot your picture
but it didn't come out
so I picture you again in my mind.
I needed a reminder
that the fetid condition of the world
is not all that is the case,
that you too are the case,
serene and wise
with nothing to grieve
save nothing to grieve.

Fiona Came By

Fiona came by today
and she smelled like sage
and oregano, rosemary and
musty delicious herbs
and she told me I looked great
(which ain't necessarily true)
and I told her she looked great
(which is true)
and we couldn't stop smiling
and alas I had about fifty emails
to answer, which I hate,
and had to cut it short
which I will regret for a long time
because what is more valuable,
answering emails or spending time
smiling with Fiona?

Piano Lessons

Parents ever tell you
"It may seem like hell now
but you'll be thankful later,
believe us"?
And of course, now
that it *is* later, you're thankful,
sure, you can play
all those etudes, mazurkas
and polonaises by Chopin
and Bach's fierce toccatas.

Your friend, Kayla, can't.
You, unlike Kayla, have
a skill, a talent, a resume boost.
Poor Kayla, while you were
practicing chaotic arpeggios
she was out getting trashed
for Mardi Gras.

Poor, Kayla, no F-sharp minors,
no key signatures, no chromatic
scales, no Chopin, no Bach.
And what does she have
to show for all that jazz
beyond the baby?

The Evanescence of Effervescence

Some strive to explicate the inexplicable human condition
by plunging into the infinitesimal ocean of quarks
while others soar toward the edges of the universe,
red-shifting motes in a star beam as they traverse . . .

plucking out the music of the spheres on a banjo

and why bother, knowing all along that we can never finally
and fully cry eureka! that what is not and never has been known
can never be known because we cannot escape the scaffolding,
the architecture, the hangman's noose, the playing field,
to gaze upon our strange selves outside of ourselves.

Leave it to some scraggly poet to chip in with another homely
     metaphor:
our ephemeral lives evaporate like the fizz in your carbonated
     sodas—
sprightly as tiny John Phillip Sousa ditties, brief yet Fourth of
     Julyish,
gas escaping, the froth of an Atlantic wave churning onto the shore
of the New World, fleeting razzmatazz, razzle-dazzle, dizzying
     leptons
crashing against a ziggurat of stalwart bosons . . .

ah, I crave the champagne, Louie, even when it goes flat—
which I've heard some savor.

Suzy

. . .& I said "Yeah
but you ain't seen Suzy . . ."
        —Everette Maddox

yes I have, old friend, in my dreams
& on the street & at the mall
& drive-in & at mardi gras
& sipping a ramos gin fizz
at the napoleon house
I've seen Suzy everywhere
which is rare
because the likes of Suzy—
"pretty as moonshine
through a broken bottle,"
you said—
is beyond compare
&, forgive me,
christ of new orleans,
I believe that once
I held her in my arms
near bayou sauvage.

The Big Picture—Smelling the Roses

That ten-second sniff of pleasure
in a fifteen-billion-year-old universe.

Where You Are

Say you're rooted in Bogalusa
But dream of Saskatoon or Yuma
Or Laramie because, well, all seem better
Than where you are. Or maybe
You're settled in a sultry Maltese village
But yearn for Truth of Consequences
Or Bangor or ancient Carthage.
Any place seems better,
Luxor. Sao Tomé. Siam. Pascagoula.
Goochland. St. Bart's. Macedonia...
Everyplace seems better than where you are
Because everyplace *is* better
Until you get there and that place
Becomes where you are.

Ignorance

Note how if you repeat a word, any word,
Say, *Geronimo* or *exegesis* or *violin,*
Repeat it in your mind, even aloud,
It will gradually drain of meaning,
An empty signifier in a vacuum,
Wine leaking from a sieve
Or soul from body
And you're left with a mere husk
While outside crows shriek,
Suction thucks, the microwave bleeps
And all is well
As if the lexicon
Were all along a necropolis
And we didn't know it,
Deemed it damn near holy.

Double Negative

Sometimes it plunges home the point
as in "I almost wasn't there no more"
with an urgency that meek, powdery "any"
misses altogether. Or my old friend
collapsed, pounding on the ground,
crying "I ain't got no love." This too
is poetry, the barbaric yawp, purer
than any tepid tally-ho or good show. . .
the rusted anvil poking out of a peat bog
alongside blackened, ossified corpses
that we must think remember at least
a rainbow or butterfly or will-o'-the-wisp,
anything airy, diaphanous, ephemeral
to defy the stolid cinder block
of *no*.

Heavenly Blues

Never the same of course,
Though hope, always newborn,
Glides smoothly into place like ambergris,
And you see not a heap of ashes,
Not the frayed curtain
Or rotten porch, but what you remember,
Always more real than the ragged blackbird
Perched on a wire, sadness reduced
To the comical shrunken head
Hawked in voodoo shops.

Yet time sings sweetly
Like the river that is never the same
As you float out of its mist
Into a hovel of specks,
Motes and figments;
You gather with roses and palmettos,
And dream softly, freezing the moment
Into a slippery opal of desire.

Kilroy Wasn't Here

The young ones don't remember me—
Who would have thought?
I was everywhere, like air,
And left my charred mark.
They all knew me
And I knew them all—
What a time we had.
Even when the war was done.
Now I'm not here, not dead
Just, somehow, unknown,
Without a tomb, forgotten.

April is the Cruelest Month

This one certainly is what with its blitzing forward fast,
Dragging behind it the entire twentieth-first century
At full speed, a crazed tug boat. It's only appropriate
I should run circles in the room and yank my skull hair out
As the hairs on my arms stand upright in alarm and dismay
At the insane pace—why, I just got out of bed one morning
In 1999, popped a Tart, sipped some Café du Monde,
And now look! Almost twenty-twenty, a decade
Of perfect vision however blind. What happened in 2002
Or 2009—did they slip by unnoticed with not even a wink
    goodbye?
Didn't we last night light a few cherry bombs to celebrate
The millennium? Where'd the millennium go? I think maybe
It didn't really happen, a dream of sorts or nightmare.
Who can bear the onslaught? Miles to go before . . .
Miles? Sleep? Desist, Tempus, whore of not Babylon,
Our personal empires, taking us for everything we've got,
That meager glut, crumbling grout, groping us good and out.

What Words Do

Before the word "fish" came to mind
I dove into the murky pond
and caught a shimmering thing
with my fingers, bit into it
and it tasted good . . .

now, eons later, I feel hungry,
hungry for fish,
and thus drive to Kroger
and pick out filet of trout
from the refrigerated case
and it still tastes good
but not as good.

Asia

I leafed through *The Tibetan Book of the Dead*
and the *I Ching,* refused to tackle Aurobindo
but perused the dialogs between Krishnamurti
and British astrophysicist David Bohm—
and to what end?
A few notes jotted on my ruled pad
that I knew I would toss into the trash
once I tired of looking at my own handwriting
which has become a chaos of tiny, fuzzy rhizomes
even I cannot decipher.
So, goodbye Asia, hardly got to know ye.

I long to etch wisdom into the gray matter
of my brain so it won't be lost
and of course with immaculate penmanship.
Is the neo-cortex our enemy or friend?
The Asians want to blot it out entirely
and subsume themselves in a cloud
of transcendence that reduces the puny ego
to the order of insect or worse, toxic microbe.

I could go for it. I was there once, down South
in the Seven Seas Bar where they served
ouzo by the barrel. And let me tell you
I found myself everywhere in Asia all at once—
looked Asia in the spectacular almond eyes.
But she dissolved and I wound up on the floor
of the latrine, throwing up the Western World.

Back home I gave up philosophy and sought
every honeysuckle in the neighborhood and,
lo, everywhere I turned they blossomed.
I sipped their nectar clean.

I Placed a Bone in Arkansas

with apologies to Wallace Stevens

I placed a bone in Arkansas
And long it was and trim and spare,
but not a bone on which to gnaw—
it lost its marrow long before.
Some time went by and I went back
to check upon that dried-up bone
and, lo, I saw a hairline crack
for which we all shall soon atone.
You cannot plant what's dead by law
and hope that it will resurrect;
once wrecked it's always, ever wrecked
like everything in Arkansas.

Dream

I tried to tell her she did not smell
like mosquito repellant
but I knew by her frown . . .
and the way she flicked her hair
that she didn't believe me.
She kept sniffing at her arms
in a kind of minor horror.
I took her hand and tried to
pull her into the house
but she resisted:"How can I
come in when I smell like poison?"
she whimpered.
"Smell me," she demanded,
"all over," as she proceeded
to remove her clothing.
What a dilemma.
If I told her she smelled
like champagne or the attar
of roses, she would accuse
me of lying;
if I told her she did indeed
smell like mosquito repellant
she would go berserk—
for this was one clean woman.
In the end I offered to rub her down
with denatured alcohol
(which smells horrible)
to remove every trace of repellant.
She liked the idea
and followed me into the house,
the screen door banging behind us.
I smeared the wretched alcohol
all over her flesh and rubbed it in.

Then I carried her to the tub
and washed it off with Ivory.
Now I'm boiling water for
sassafras tea as she lies back
on the sofa, smiling, purified,
ablated, redeemed.
And I tell you, I'm smiling too.

Daisy and Ritz Crackers

We had stationed her bed beside the back room
love seat. Arthritis and organ failure had set it
and she could hardly move. But whenever
I appeared the next morning in the kitchen doorway
rooting in the box for another Ritz Cracker
she struggled to stand precariously, to wag
her tail slowly, heavily, as if the energy
it required was too much. She would hobble over
though I would have brought it to her—
and waited for my cracker-pinched fingers
to make the offering. Had to be careful
because she could still take a chunk of hand
as her jaws clamped down. So happy
she was to wolf down those orange wafers.
And I so sad. Take and eat, Daisy.

Brass

Three for My Father

I. Sears Nights

Back then I would ride with my dad
Over to Sears in the Gentilly East mall,
Already run-down, shoddy and sad.
Katrina would finish it off years later.
I realize now that Dad had no reason
To make those drives other than
Wanting to get away for a spell.

He tinkered with the bins of screws and bolts,
Rubbed them between his fingers as if to test
Their reality. He didn't really need them
But always bought a few, though
He loved carriage bolts and brass flanges
And stored them in wooden cigar boxes.
This was before Lowe's and Home Depot
When Sears actually sold single screws
And nuts and washers, grommets and wire.

Later we might cross the street
To FrosTop and drink those icy mugs
Of root beer that tasted like Castoria.
Dad liked to run the car with the wipers on
Even when it wasn't raining. As he sipped
He would hum some Mozart motet to the beat
Of those wipers. We didn't talk much.

There was a night club called Pussy Cat Lounge
Right next to FrosTop, but it would be
A while before my friends and I ventured there.
At the time it seemed evil to me
With its multi-colored neon insignia
Of a glass of champagne, complete

With bubbles evaporating above.
One time I saw a woman strut in,
A cigarette dangling from her lip,
A woman I might have died for
Only a few years later. Dad noticed too.
I watched his eyes follow her
in the rearview as she approached.
This is how largesse comes into and goes
From our lives, in glances, reflections,
Momentary glimpses.

Dad, I'm speaking to you now in a way
I didn't then. Because the memory of Sears
And those ridiculous screws and bolts
Suddenly popped into my mind like
One of Pussycat's champagne bubbles—
and it's already dissolving.
I want to tell you how much I liked
Those drives, away from homework, weeknights,
Mom and Ruthie, waiting for us with a plate
Of hot cross buns, molten sugar dripping
Down the sides of dough, stupid TV shows.

You can't buy single wood screws anymore
And those pre-packaged are half plastic.
The heads strip unless you go really slow
And aim that driver squarely into a groove.
You told me once that things don't change,
They thicken. Well, can't say I agree.
I think they melt. But I know what you meant.

II. Relish

Once at Coney Island I devoured
a foot-long hot dog with relish
though since then I have sworn off
wieners, Hebrew or otherwise,
with or without relish, yet still
the idea "with relish" prompts me
to assault the daily routines of washing,
dusting, cleaning, repairing, driving, discarding
with relish, the surfeit of dailiness,
as I once relished that dog loaded
with onions, chili, crushed pickles, mustard,
all of which transformed a bland white bun
into something almost holy, a Eucharistic feast.

After all, I was fourteen and on the move,
seeking thrills, and just about to board
The Cyclone, and after that, the Parachute Jump,
which, while harnessed, dropped us kids
straight down at least two hundred feet
with the expected jolt to the system
when we landed.
                      Even then I knew
"with relish" implied its opposite.
Too young to grasp diminishment
as it might apply to me, I spotted
from that height my father on the boardwalk.
He leaned against a wooden rail smoking
one of his beloved Picayunes. He looked
small, distant, not unhappy but not happy
as he waited for me to descend, charge
over to him with the relish of one who had
survived a thrilling ordeal. I saw it in his eyes:

diminishment, never again to submit himself
to the pure excitement of free fall.
I asked him if he wanted a hot dog—
they're great, I exclaimed—he shook his head
and complained of heartburn. Too rich,
he said, all that relish.
                              It will become
the Age of White Bread soon enough
I must have understood—but at the time
refused to understand. We sat on a bench
watching some ragged pigeons pecking
at crumbs in the dirt.

III. Syllogism
    for my father

I turned nineteen that summer,
a year of college already aced,
a new car and sizzling girlfriend—
nothing slowed me down.
I knew it all, had it all.
So forgive me
if I couldn't work up much fire
about loading furniture into a rented truck
with my father, who offered to help.

Dad was ok . . . but I was nineteen.
Sometimes he got on my nerves.
He hadn't gone beyond high school
so I figured I was the one
with all the answers now.
I told him about the philosophy course
Freshmen were required to take,

42

how we learned about thinking
and the structure of logic.
That sounded good, I thought,
"The structure of logic."
I told him Socrates was a man
and all men were mortal.
so Socrates was mortal.
"Who doesn't know that?" he laughed
as we struggled with a sleeper-sofa
that seemed welded in place.
"It's called a syllogism," I said.

A fuzzy image of the teacher, Dr. Bleen,
floated through my mind like seaweed.
He wore baggy corduroy jackets
with leather elbow patches,
propped his feet on an antique desk in class
and smoked an aromatic pipe.
His hands were smooth as cream,
unlike Dad's, who could never scrub off
all the paint, stain and scars.
I couldn't imagine Dr. Bleen
helping me stuff furniture into a U-Haul.
"What was that word?" Dad asked,
sadness weighing his voice.
"Syllogism," I said.
"Funny word . . . and it means so much?"

We finally managed to slide the sofa
all the way back toward the cab.
New Orleans in August is merciless;
we were both drenched, gasping for air.
Something then released itself in my head.
Blood dripped from my nose like broth.

"Jesus!" my father cried.
I staggered to the ramp to sit and dab
at my nostrils with his handkerchief.
"You ok? Just a nose bleed probably."
Later he told me I turned milk-white
hunched on that fluted, aluminum ramp.
None of the furniture we moved still exists,
they've probably recycled the truck
and Dad too is gone.
Only that instant of terror remains,
relish. I still taste it—
with a different tongue.

Remembering and Forgetting

Why do we remember what we remember
and forget what we forget?
I'm not talking about the big things, say,
the time you broke your arm
or Uncle Ambrose had a stroke, no,
we remember that grand stuff well enough,
I'm talking about the petty little nothings
that for whatever reason return at odd times
like when you're raking leaves or
scrubbing the kitchen sink or toilet,
how some incidental person's face will
suddenly return or not return, someone
you barely knew, encountered once and
maybe for only fifteen minutes,
someone who didn't impress you much
one way or another . . .

yet that face persists as if embedded
in the concrete of gray matter,
a kind of memento mori, a keepsake
for the whatnot, a useless image or byte
or information like that formula I learned
as an undergrad about how fast a snowball
will melt if you are stationed five feet
from a brick wall and equipped with its
angular momentum, speed and density.

Why should I remember that and not the face
of that wonderful girl who took me for a spin
in her red Fiat Spider?
It's as if memory amounts to mere pastiche,
a partial you, a tapestry riddled with holes—
and what we forget, where does it go
and what mighty shovel might excavate it?

How much of yesterday have you forgotten?
Which parts do you remember?
And who remembers you being there
tomorrow?

Same Ole

Ever feel you're getting nowhere
because the usual exigencies—mailing out bills,
draping your shirts on hangers, scrubbing the toilet,
deciding what to eat tonight (you know, the usual
everyday) hold you back so that instead of heading
for Yuma to find the woman in the pillbox hat
who threatened to kill you on a Greyhound bus
en route to San Francisco (where you first read Marquez)
or sneaking over to the Yucatan with Gretchen
from Bavaria, instead of something new and thrilling
you find yourself holed up in the house vacuuming
debris from the carpet of scrubbing the hardened
remains of tomato sauce from a pot or spraying
for spiders?

Ever want to slide behind the wheel
and just drive until the gas runs out—even if you're
stranded in Beeville, Texas, at one hundred degrees
in the shade, no bills, no pesos, no nothing, just
you in a damp sombrero, scampering after a Gila monster
because you're hungry and will eat anything—
cactus tastes pretty good once you pull out the spikes.
The phone messages accrue but you don't want to talk
to anybody, especially that chirpy one who informs
you that you've won a grand cruise to Somalia.
She keeps calling, so does BankAmericard with news
of better interest rate (fifty percent, not eighty),
ever want to smash the landline with that sledge
hammer out in the shed—and toss the cell into
some lagoon in Barataria?

Why is it all too much?
A surgeon general once reported that it's not the big
stuff that exponentializes stress—divorce, deaths
of friends, the house collapsing—it's the accumulation
of micro-horrors, scrubbing that spaghetti sauce
from the pot for the thousandth time, raking
the half-dead lawn, the usual . . . nice to embark
on something new—"Lady in pillbox hat, why'd
you threaten to kill me? Can I buy you a drink?"
Gretchen from Bavaria, meet me not in Yucatan
but Colorado Springs, you know, for the medicinal pot.
Otherwise, I'm not game for much these days—
that sauce, now petrified, ineradicable:
I refuse to scour it away one more time.

You're Beautiful

We're in Galatoire's and I watch
you nibble the shrimp remoulade
with some regret and not a little nausea.
I don't like you. The feeling is mutual
but here we are. I brought you here
because you're beautiful and everyone
needs a dose of beauty in the otherwise
miasma of passing time. What does
that say about me? I presume the worst.
And though it's my stupid peccadillo
I can't stand to watch girls eat meat
of any kind. They should eat flowers.

Hitler said eating meat is eating a corpse.
Not that I admire Hitler, though they
say he loved children and always smelled
like soap. From here we'll stroll up Bourbon
and head over to the Napoleon House
for bad Ramos Gin Fizzes—or maybe
a few shots of yellow chartreuse.
Someone will have slid Debussy onto
the turntable, and you will stare
at the ceiling. I still don't like you.

This is where they wanted to sequester
Napoleon after his rescue from St. Helena's—
it didn't work out. And who knows
what's true or false anymore?
Maybe I love you, I don't know, but
it's pretty feeble to love someone
because they're beautiful. I know
some pretty evil beautiful people.

And you just sit there at the table
sipping a strawberry daiquiri, that
blank look on your face. You hate me.

Why are we here together? Napoleon
lost Waterloo because his hemorrhoids
flared, not because Wellington
was a better tactician. I don't tell you
any of this because you would sigh.
I don't tell you anything. You don't
tell me anything. We're miserable.
God, you're beautiful.

Absolute Cafe

That time we trekked over to the
Absolute Cafe in olde uptown New Orleans
for something sweet after the long drive,
to slouch, lean back and relax, not pay
attention for a while . . .
but suddenly you screamed, maniacally
brushed your hair, stretched fingers
down your back, sweeping whatever it was
away

the moon was full, the midnight crisp,
we had half-finished our cheesecakes,
you strawberry, mine plain, ah, so
delicious, so needed . . .
and now mayhem, pain, something
had bitten you and flaming welts
blossomed on your young, fair skin,
all over, no doubt a spider

I rushed into the all-night grocery
next door and bought a bottle of
Benadryl and also the lotion version
and I rubbed the salve into your skin
right then and there as you sipped
two adult portions of the drinkable
version

that moment has never left me,
you looked terrified, turned pale,
and yet remained beautiful in
that extremis . . . that's what I
remember most, how beautiful
you looked, even when desperate,

and how desperate I was to
assuage you

I, seeker of omens, continue
to wonder what it meant, that
outrage, that beast of the night
springing without cause
and I recall Blake's invisible worm
flying through the night to assail
the rose with its dark, secret love

Scherzo Furiant—America Now

I listen to the glorious fourth movement
of the Sixth Symphony and wonder
what the hell Anton Dvorak was doing
in Spillsville, Iowa, in 1893.
Kolaces, polkas, pilsener…
he loved the place and listened
as the Dubuque Symphony performed
The New World in a high school gym.
He fished in the Turkey River
and instructed Americans that
they had better heed black and
native American music:
there was the soul of the USA.
In the end he missed Bohemia
and returned home to the ancient,
surreal, tragic, passionate origin
of Czechoslovakia.
      Sometimes I wonder what I too
am doing in America, especially now.
I have no Czech accouterments
except a few pair of old glass
Mardi Gras beads crafted in that country
decades ago. Or make it some stone,
solemn church in Armenia where
women in black shawls rub their rosaries
in avid precision. No scherzo furiant—
only centuries of mute grief.
Grave New World.

Another Small Good Thing

After finishing my own moseying about
in the mall I settle myself on a cushioned bench
next to the massive stone fireplace
where I await the return of my wife and daughters.
A sweet, calm little respite spot it is—
ladies with babies, old men in rockers,
teenagers who can't keep their hands off each other.
About twenty yards hither, the main walkway
with its usual promenade of shoppers.

And here comes a family of three—mother,
dad and tyke of about four years old.
I am watching everyone and no one at once.
But this tyke, cropped blond hair, a kind
of jump suit . . . a happy kid . . .
he catches my eye and commences to zoom
over toward me, big smile on his face
(why? I've never seen him before).
He approaches and gently touches my knee
with his little fingers. "Hello," I smile back.
The father rushes over and scoops him up
and they disappear.

I feel really good about the incident
and take it as an omen of beatitude.
If only we could all rush about touching
each other's knees!
But then, he's little, he's innocent—
he will soon be educated out of such kind,
compassionate risks.

Once In Ur

Once in Ur I met a girl who sold
kumquats from a basket strapped
to her mule—oh, it was a frightful season
then, no rain for months, her lips
cracked, we all swatted away
the flies and blowing sand and
children danced for a storm.
I, a merchant, in Ur for the business
and perhaps on a secret diplomatic
mission for my king in Phrygia,
I was used to the wenches and
had my share, though weary now
of constant disarray. But
I fell in love with the girl in Ur—
how bright her avocado eyes,
how wheaty the amber hair the tips
of which draped and lightly touched
her slender shoulders.
You doubt love at first sight
and pass it off as lust? Well,
think what you may—but this I know:
the girl from Ur smiled at me
and lured me in and thereupon
we eloped in all of Asia Minor.

I see your cup is empty, my friend.
Allow me to pour you more of this
legendary Abyssinian fig and date wine,
a favorite of Xerxes the Great.
When you love a woman—and I know
you say you love Naxinia, or think you do—
when you love a woman you want her
to want to bear your child; you want
to get her with child; because it's

the closest you can ever conjoin with her,
when two become one, then three.
You and Naxinia remain barren, true?
Let this be my testament thereupon:
Eros looks backward from the future,
incarnates past ecstasy in such fruit.

Encounter Upon A Hike

I trekked the path beside the river
and came to a bend beyond which
sojourners cannot see where they began
because of thick underbrush,
the stand of low-branched pines.
No one much goes this far and we've heard
reports that it might be dangerous after dark.

Well, it wasn't dark yet but near it.
Up about a quarter mile I came across
a fellow wayfarer, a mangled girl
who supported herself upon a walker
on wheels. Young, she was young,
too young for such affliction, whether
accident or disease. Her legs seemed
to bend and twist every which way
and it must have been quite a task
for her to so venture—and quite brave
to achieve it.

When we passed
each other she kept her eyes cast down
as if to hide away her disfigurement.
She would not meet my gaze and I
suspect, she met no one's gaze ever.
She seemed ashamed and yet, as I said,
how brave. I wanted to greet her,
pat her on the back, maybe even hug her.
But on she hobbled and I too
in the opposite direction, though
pretty soon I turned around to head back.

The girl had disappeared from view
and soon I'd come again to the bend
and civilization. Along the path
workers, I assume, had planted trees
and beside each tree a post and placard,
each latter a small metal square etched
with hieroglyphs or runes. They could not
be read by the ordinary eye. I knew quite well
what they meant: you had to scan them
with some digital device to break the code
and read some text explaining each tree.

And yet, I wondered, why such mystery?
Why not engrave the information in language
anyone to read? Here a sycamore, here
an elm, here a silver maple and there an oak
Do we no longer trust the straightforward,
the easy, the age-old exchange?
I hoped more than ever to find that lame girl
and look her in the eye.

The Best Po-Boy

Once, not in Aleppo, not Byzantium,
not stony Prague, but Bogalusa, Louisiana,
I found a corner dive, the kind decorated
with gaudy metal Coca-Cola signs
and hand-written specials on blackboard slate,
that served the best shrimp po-boys ever concocted,
hell, maybe it wasn't Bogalusa but Domilici's
on Annunciation Street. Those who indulge
know that every po-boy is different, every
chef fiddles with the ingredients and degree
of ketchup, horseradish, Tabasco . . .
the white sauces don't cut it at all.
So when you come across the Platonic
sine qua non, you slip into a gustatory sublime
and spread the gospel. It's religious, of course.

And does this not apply to just about any
summum bonum? The purpose of metaphor.
I alone am come to tell ye!
No finer woman than what's her name
down in Bogalusa way back.
Best Dodge Dart I've ever driven!
But as to what's her name, here's the glitch:
nothing else that comes along will do.
It's what's her name or nothing because
we stick with what we crave and give up
craving anything else. Whereas, we all know,
a finer sedan, a finer woman, a finer po-boy
may lie inches away around the corner.

But we won't even sniff, taste or sample.
We're buried in the tomb of nonpareil.
We know our Plato. The heavenly fix
before Heaven. I knew the man—no democrat
let me tell you. Gave him a bite of my po-boy,
let him fondle my what's her name
for a moment for the sake of comparative ecstasy.
And it's absolutes ever since, absolute misery
over what we've lost and what we refuse to
find anew. And this we call judgment.

With Jen and Sue and Bob Dylan

First time I heard Bob Dylan
and this way before marijuana
and two dead marriages and college
and grad school. . .
in those days we got drunk
and Jen's dad, a real boozer, had stocked
his refurbished basement with a bar
and whatever anyone needed.
The dad and his new wife, third marriages
for each, were out at some flamboyant
New Year's Eve party, and Jen, this
beautiful blond, for reasons
I'll never grasp, did not have a date.

She invited me and my girlfriend over
to celebrate who knows now what year.
The dad had strung twinkling lights
across the ceiling and a dried-out, ragged
Christmas tree lagged over in one corner,
limp leftover tinsel hanging sadly
from a few branches, a broken ornament
on the floor. Butter-vanilla candles
glowed serenely on the mantle
above a crackling hickory fire.
Jen poured the vodka and Sue and I
sank into the plush sofa stationed
in the middle of the room.
We got loaded fast, and so did Jen.
The dad had left on some junky
holiday music—Bing Crosby, Burl Ives,
Andy Williams,
stuff we three gagged on. Then Jen
put on the Dylan, "To Ramona,"

"Subterranean Homesick Blues,
"Just Like a Woman" . . .

And she started to dance with herself,
flinging back her long hair and caressing
herself with one hand, a glass of vodka
in the other. Oh, it was cozy and I felt so good,
One of those moments you make a point
of remembering. Dylan sank into me
like some wondrous new emotion.
I tugged Sue from the sofa and we
started to dance, real slow, dancing
to Dylan, imagine. When I peered over
at Jen she looked so wan and melancholic,
a pre-Raphaelite, forlorn woman who
seemed to melt before my eyes,
liquefy in her black rib sheath.

Sue and I inched over toward her
and the three of us danced together.
I had my arms around the waists of two
splendid girls, I who had only recently
emerged from a painful high school past.
I believe at the time we were still seniors.
ready to graduate in coming months.
I wound up dancing with Jen because Sue
felt dizzy and crashed on the sofa.
This was forbidden of course, but that dance
aroused me in a way I had never before known,
the guilt, like a sweet wound, throbbed.

She smelled up close like faint sweet olive
And all the while Sue, watching, smiling.
No threesomes in those days, nothing kinky,
and yet kink smoldered in the air like voltage

and made arousal all the more religious.
In the end everything that could have happened,
didn't. Sue and I left at dawn. Jen's parents
returned.

I was left to wonder what my illicit dream
of Jen meant. Was unfulfilled desire
greater than that fulfilled? Would there
always be another Jen on the other side
of a room dancing with herself, waiting,
molten? Would she always come to me
singing "Just Like A Woman" sweetly
in my ear as we embraced on some
preposterous future New Year?

Happy

Let's write a happy poem together.
Let's share rather than bear
the weight of our windowless monads.
Let's gather, not like nomads,
but a family of don't worry/be happy folk.
Uncle Antipasto had a stroke?
Well, what doesn't kill us makes us
stronger. The grass is always greener.
He's in a better place. He's with his dog,
Caligula, in heaven. Come on, y'all . . .
if you're happy and you know it,
clap your glands; God's in his heaven
and all's right with the world
(I really wish Browning had not said that).
If you can't say something nice
don't say anything at all. The rice
is contaminated with arsenic?
You're in good hands with Allstate.
Plague psoriasis? Take Repromene
though it may vaporize your spleen.
You can't buy happiness, no ma'am—
look at me! Joyous as a clam.
Let us engage, assess and create rubrics
soon to be made into motion pictures
by Stanley Kubrick.
Is he still alive? Doesn't matter if not:
he's in a better place, remember?
Not the bleak December
of Edgar A. Poe but the "can spring
be far behind?" Stubbed your toe?
Make every moment count.
Live for the moment. Fear no evil.
Contemplate the heart's steeple
not its blackened bogs.

Wash the car. Feed the hogs.
A penny saved is a penny spurned.
All you need is love. Kumbaya.
Groovy, man, we're blissed out.
A bird in the hand is worth two in the bush—
but look, Ma, it has the Asiatic flu.
What doesn't kill you . . .
Bring it on! Aim for the stars.
Ignore those hideous scars.
Be all you can be. Have a good day.
Now don't you feel better? Coke adds life.
Thank you so much for sharing our good cheer.
Merry Christmas and Happy New Year.

Halcyon

Remember the days when
you could toke fifteen thousand joints at a go
and steady them with an infinite succession
of vodka martinis and you memorized
Jubilate Agno because it seemed the only sane
thing to do in the madness of corporate AmeriKa?
You might be huddled in your grandmother's
art deco bathroom with its Alphonse Mucha colors
because grandmother wasn't home no more
or maybe lying flat on a mattress in a trailer
in Boone County, Missouri, when a girl
offers you a chilled glass of orange juice
and it seemed you were drinking heaven
because orange juice never tasted so good

or maybe it was in that shack on Zest street
in New Orleans and Bach blasted from your speakers
and you just knew redemption was at hand
or was it in Corrine Dunbar's on St. Charles
when you and Allegra (not the antihistamine)
ordered a full course meal with no money
in your pockets, oh, she was Byron's daughter
all right, and you both passed out in the taxi
home after fleeing the restaurant with bloodhounds
on your heels? Remember those days? Do
they now seen an eyeblink or an eternity away?
Do you wonder like an imbecile what happened?
What happened? What happened? What happened?

And of course it's all too obvious because now
you have moved from psychedelic to psychopathic,
a trip you never registered for, could never
have imagined, cruise or no cruise, and you
wouldn't trade places with Kit Smart for all
the gold in Californ though that gold could buy
you another past, another you, more gold
since money begets money . . .
but you also know that to answer your own question
would mean the real and final Fall from Eden,
another dilapidated bardo and some cardboard box
on the curb. So you let it be, bask in ignorance
and watch another re-run of Dante's *Inferno*.

Edgar Allan Poe Meets Paris Hilton

Nothing like Lenore but since I'm dead
(rabies they now say) I can't be picky.
Staggered my way into this ritzy party
at the Chelsea where, despite the grunge,
the hip crowd gathers. They tell me
Thomas Wolfe lived here for a while.
Who's Thomas Wolfe? You miss out
on so much when you die. Anyway,
there she stood in a sort of neon nimbus
eyes half-closed as if high on laudanum
or whatever they use these days, that
subtle smile, no doubt she's sexy
in a kittenish way (nothing like my
smoldering Lenore) . . .chatting with
some blond tycoon, a martini dangling
from her delicate hand (some sort
of defiance of gravity here which I
must remember to note in the next
edition of *Eureka.)* So I moved in on them
and tycoon quickly vanished. I know
I looked shabby next to her (how I miss
Virginia) but when you're desperate
you make desperate mistakes.
The slit eyes widened—she had never
seen the likes of anything like me.
I told her I wrote "The Raven" because
that usually works, but she had never
heard of it. Never heard of the most
famous poem in the New World?
Bodes no good. She tried to turn away
but I informed her that I was dead.

"Well, that's interesting," she smiled,
took my hand and led me up the stairs.
"Come on, silly man," she purred,
let me put you on YouTube."

Mr. Jimmy

I went down to the Chelsea drugstore
To have your prescription filled
I was standing in line with Mr. Jimmy
And man did he look pretty ill. . .
                    —Rolling Stones

No doubt we all have a Mr. Jimmy
somewhere in our historic blitz.
My Mr. Jimmy owned a neighborhood
hardware store sandwiched between
a drugstore and barber shop.
Faded wooden planks, the floor,
a small wooden counter atop which
sat an ornate brass noveau cash register.
The place was dim, illuminated by
a single bulb dangling from a frayed wire.
In sweltering summers a battered space fan
vibrated on the uneven planks.

Behind the counter, endless pigeonholes
full of screws, nails, tacks, carriage bolts,
fasteners, clasps . . . anything you wanted.
Further back, the tools, paint, lawn mowers.
You could buy a single screw, a single nail
unlike now when Lowe's and Home Depot
package it all by the dozens.
Mr. Jimmy, a tall, lank, pale man,
friendly in a Norman Rockwell manner,
made his living with that quaint business
but he saw the future, the franchises,
the mega-emporiums.
First the drugstore closed then the barber died,

soon Mr. Jimmy shut down and faded
out of time. I believe my dad bought
the last screw he sold in that place.
He bought it as a feeble gesture.
It cost a penny. He kept that screw
in his pocket for many years.

Au Lecteur

for Eric

I listen to Rachmaninoff's Second Piano Concerto
as I wait in the parking slot of King Buffet
for my friend Eric who has just returned from Paris
and I from Knoxville.
We have so met here for years to sip egg drop soup
and what passes for Chinese food, greasy, salty
chicken with broccoli, fake seafood salad, green
beans, tiny stuffed crabs . . .
but the real feast is the talk, the communion,
the recent photographs.

A second-rate Rachmaninoff it was
but anyone who can play it period gets my vote.
Who can define melody? How does mind
create it? Is it remembered as are words?
Eric reads a first stanza of Baudelaire for me
in French—the damned r's and gutturals
confound me, remind me of one's attempt
to throw up. But I have read much Rimbaud
and Baudelaire lately—the latter's angst, poignant,
Rimbaud's morbidity and nastiness, refreshing.
It occurs to me that without art, without music,
poetry, paintings, we are all doomed to malaise,
mediocrity, bland, tepid similacritude
(is there such a word? there should be).

Mon frere, it is good to see you again.
It is good to talk about what we love.
I tell him that I've just discovered Victor Hugo's poems
which prompts a rhapsodic spiel on Hugo's
life, fame, progeny—and grandiose funeral.

He reminds me that I introduced him to Walker Percy
and John Cheever whose prose styles he describes
as "delicious." He is fluent in both languages,
I mired in this one, though I once aced
the Princeton standardized test in French.
So much for standardized tests.

Some people we know we've known all our lives
at first meeting. You know who they are.
I think the key is passion, a new melody,
crests with no troughs. Friend, you visited me
when I lay in a hospital with broken ribs;
you transported me and Cathy back home
over that wretched mountain you call a hill;
you taxied our girls back from Wake Forest.
Merci . . . oh, how young we were once.
J'ai plus souvenirs que si l'avais mille ans.

Percussion

Lament for my Student who Took His Own Life

It's been a while now, David. I no longer
count years; years are now jumbled smears
behind, and I assume before me—and no
doubt you too, for you are infinitely older
than I am now.

                I first learned of your death
when Parks called with the news. How can I
describe that moment? A caving in of self,
a St. Vitus dance of the brain. the sudden
expulsion from here & now? You aimed
for your heart not brain, and I understand why.
I don't want this to become another hackneyed
tribute to the dead though I've come to suspect
that all such tributes are hackneyed. But
it seems the usual.They put you on medications
that prompted your already legion demons
to multiply and attack . . .and, soldier, you
Romanized the onslaught, sensing
intolerable odds, and fell upon your sword,
so to speak.

In your book *Regret for Breakfast* you wrote:
"Fear is understanding/Why madness can be normal. . . ."
and while I knew that you were never "normal"
(what poet is?), I failed to grasp your depths.
How I could have helped I don't know.
I do know that your death was outrageous,
that once again we all lost a prince who should be
right now at the pinnacle of triumph.
It's taken me a while to write this; I've tried
before. Because I think of you often

and when I do it's under the magnolia
across from Young Hall, the rest of the class
dispersed, and only you, Courtney and I
lingering to talk about poetry, which means
talking about everything. You two, young
and vibrant, sitting on the grass, backs
against the brick wall, I already in my lawn
chair given my brittle chakras.
It's as it that moment has preserved itself
in the amber of my mind.

      The last time I saw you was at your
grandmother's funeral, I think grandmother
anyway, the one you loved most. (I don't
recall if Rita was still alive then or not—as I said,
it's all smear these days.) You had taken
to bodybuilding, had leapt out of your
previous guises and bulged with youth, smiles
and confidence. And for whatever small part
I played in your life, I felt proud.
And you wrote; "I don't reckon it matters/
but when I think about what's true/
or what's not/I don't waste time/foolin' myself."

Prayer

Dear God, if you don't exist, please listen anyway.
Nothing Vesuvian tonight, just another day, you know,
inanimate objects rebelling simultaneously or
in tandem . . . when I tried to yank open a closet door
the knob fell off onto my bad toe; every Pilot pen I own
ran out of ink, so I had to slit my wrist, pluck a feather
from the dove outside and write my to-do list for tomorrow
in blood, tomorrow, which, given your gracious mercy,
you will allow to unfold, although I would understand
if you changed your mind about tomorrow, for surely
tomorrows are finite and must end at some point,
like tomorrow.

But why did fifteen light bulbs burn out at once?
Why did the hive on my shoulder expand to take
the shape of Louisiana? And so much more, in tandem
as I said, forgive my repetitions . . . silverfish
devoured a crucial page in my first edition
of Wallace's *Infinite Jest* (which, forgive me, I shall
never read), but still . . . why has winter persisted
for so long? why did I lose a crisp new Ben Franklin
in the Walmart parking lot? why did the main sewer line
erupt? why has the full moon disappeared right when
I made time to observe it? why are we contaminating
the planet with plastics and insecticides and plutonium
and why is the Ukraine exploding and why so much slaughter
in Syria and why is the Milky Way expanding and why
will the universe, in a greater tomorrow, God willing,
why is the universe doomed to a "heat death"
which will stifle all atomic motion, like a battery
drained of juice (and, Sir or Madame, regard the implications
of that scenario . . .

. . .) what was the purpose of Homer
and Dante and Shakespeare and Mozart and Bach
if they too, with the universe, cease to exist along with it?
Why did my grandfather go senile and my father
burst a vein in his brain? Why did that kid on my block
so long ago contract polio and wind up in a wheelchair?
But, I promised, nothing major here, mere tidbits,
mere weariness and ennui, nothing seismic, no, I promised . . .
so why can I never make the full leap into your largesse
and why must you be so outrageous and aloof?
Why have you not answered my emails? And yet,
and yet, here I am again, panting perhaps, desperate
for Thy "like" on Facebook, terrified that You do not
exist and have never existed even as I sincerely trust
in You and believe You must exist, whether You do
or not, for either is equally preposterous. Amen.

House on Fire

When the house down the street burst into flames
I thought of Heraclitus, that mean-tempered, mystic man.
Smoke coiled and fire forked from the roof
and the town blared with sirens.
All is flux, true, all conflict, and out of conflict's ashes
the phoenix rises. Plato looked the other way,
sought the fixed, rigid eternal and thus
condemned himself to longing.
I watched firefighters toss down smoking shards
from the charred, blackened roof
into the virgin snow blanketing our streets.
A holy alliance of opposites, the day's metaphor.
And tomorrow's forecast: ice.
Thales was the waterman, but ice, Platonic water.
A house burns on the Chinese New Year,
Year of The (snow-colored) Sheep.
What sort of omen have we here?
I felt my heart delve as I watched fire consume
that house, any house, anybody, Buddhist monks,
the ghastly phoenix returning for more.
The way is not the way, the view is not the view,
the truth not the truth, beauty not beauty—
and yet some mangled beauty or truth
or direction squirms out of the soot.

The Workers

The workmen outside have been at it all day
digging up the street with jackhammers,
backhoes and Deere machines I can't name
though which, if fitted with flesh and blood,
would resemble dinosaurs, a stegosaurus maybe
and certainly T-rex. They handle the monstrous
machines deftly and with a grace I can only envy.
They're going down deep into the street
toward the pipes, pumping out bilge and brackish
filth, a chthonian venture, linked close to hell.
The workers wear hard hats and filthy clothes;
they dig in the rain, at night the moon
coats them with luminous silt, under the blazing sun
they sweat heroically. They never seem to tire
or gripe about the arduous drone of their lives.

When I step out onto the porch, trek down the steps
and head toward my van parked on that street,
a thick book of poetry wedged between my arm and chest,
they stare briefly as I stare briefly at them.
They, of course, are the poems
not anthologized in my book, the honest poems,
not the morose, maudlin, cynical, gloomy poems
I have read all my life and passed on to students.
I steer carefully between machines, roll over
a thick hose, and edge past the detour sign.
Tomorrow, I've heard, the workers will move on
to another street   they've finished the job here.
My book presses hard against my ribs.

Sharks and Alligators

for Cat

Sharks and alligators, these your horror demons.
They fascinated you, you studied them,
could not pry you from the set during *Shark Week*.
You dream of them, for a while sharks disguised
as Buddhist monks. I have yet to decipher
though must have something to do with the bestiality
of religion or perhaps you have swooned into
your own reptilian brain and maybe mine,
everybody's. We gazed at the massive white croc
in the New Orleans Aquarium, stunned, appalled
at its immobility, its telling eyes, its tonnage.
Bought silly replicas in the souvenir shop
one of which now props atop the microwave,
a rubber cartoon with red eyes.
The albino we learned was sterile, found
in the swamps, only a few of its kind.
Pollution, no doubt, but who knows.

I think it has died since we last witnessed.
My sister once painted a picture of that white beast
under the bed of a sleeping child covered with
patchwork quilts, a tidy, bright room.
I wanted that painting but Katrina destroyed it.
The original Choctaw name of New Orleans
is Chinchaga, which means alligator.
After Katrina when we took the girls
to the Audubon Park lagoon to feed the ducks,
as our usual habit, no ducks left, only a single black swan
until some weird reptiles popped their heads
out of the bilge to receive our bread.

At first we thought turtles. But no, the heads
were baby gators. You shrieked, *the mother*
must be around. We must leave right now.
And leave we did. Rumor had it that gators
had eaten all the ducks, that they found gators
in the floodwaters that submerged the streets,
that gators had devoured a drowned priest.
Priest. Buddhist monks. Were you on to something
primordial, a dream body of apocalyptic mayhem?
Fear held me back but you plunged straight
into that maelstrom, that dark bog of the mind.

Sugie, When You Coming to Get That Turkey?

I'm in love with the message
on my mother's answering machine—
from Aunt Sylvia, my god-mother,
who describes the headaches
that now blacken her every waking moment
as tarantulas.
No *impacted,* no *empowered*—
just words raw and sweet as gizzards,
poetry, if poetry means
a flash of heightened economy
tempered by beauty,
and easy, said Keats, like leaves on a tree.

I'm alone in the house on a visit.
My mother, almost seventy-five,
is out prowling for the right vanilla bean,
the secret of her legendary bread pudding.
She'll park the yolk-colored Hyundai
and walk a dozen or more blocks
to Central Grocery on Decatur Street
then zoom over to Delchamp's
for Carnation condensed milk,
a syrup so perfect it seems holy.
Somewhere else for French bread
not quite stale enough to throw away,
another secret.
At her age I will huddle in a corner
and stare at some lonely candle.

Aunt Sylvia, the oldest of three girls,
demanded and received homage in her day
but time has faded her severe perfume.
One night twenty years ago, as she lay asleep,
something yanked the quilt from her bed

and prodded her ribs with soft talons.
It scampered over the mattress
and leapt onto my grandfather
who slept on the other side of the same room.
He jolted up, staggered to the bathroom,
sat on the tub's edge and smoked a White Owl.
Goblins, she called them, for they came often
after that night, ransacking the covers,
jabbing playfully at her bones.
My grandfather said they tickled his face
like moth wings.

The house is haunted, my mother said.
I was out of town when Paw
drowned in a puddle of his own blood.
The turkey carcass floats on a platter
in Sylvia's refrigerator, bound in layers
of Saran Wrap and aluminum foil.
My mother will carve out anything useful,
freeze the parts in plastic containers
and cook the skeleton for broth.
Its ghost will rejoice
at such impeccable annihilation.
No remnant of gross flesh will survive
to remind it of either horror or joy.

I burden this chair like an anchor,
listen to the message again.
Sugie, when you coming to get that turkey?
Sylvia's head crawls with spiders.
My mother opens the blinds.
It's too dark, she scolds;

I'll boil some water. Inhale the steam.
Those goblins haven't come for years,
Sylvia moans, *not since Daddy.*
But that's not what killed him.
Sugie . . .
I press re-play over and over.
I can't move, the phone rings, I don't answer.
Honey, you there? Did anyone call?
I'm at Sylvia's. Be back soon.
Not long ago I sat here
during a break from our hospital vigil
after a vein in my own father's head exploded.
Spirits roared through the room
like a maelstrom and I fled outside
to lean against the towering bay leaf tree,
panting.
Sugie, when you coming?
We'll have turkey soup tonight,
bread pudding for dessert.
Tarantulas gather at the windows.
Sweet cream drips from skull sockets,
cracks in the jaw. Imagine! So much blood,
so few words, a few paltry secrets.
Smoke rises from the wick of this candle
like a wishbone. *Sugie.*

Life as We Don't Know It

The technos are now working on what they call
a quantum computer which will eliminate
the 1/0 either/or business once and for all.
But get this: to do so the operating system
must be chilled to near absolute zero.
The only other place in the universe this cold
is somewhere out in something called
The Boomerang Galaxy. By tapping into
quanta the computer can perform
millions of operations at the same time,
sort of like what you do when multi-tasking,
except it would be countless you's
tasking multiple multiples.

This machine (can we even call it "machine"?)
works by tapping into a parallel universe!
Whoever emails on it may wind up
in another cosmos! This is no joke.
All based upon something called,
and what a wonderful name, "The
Collapse of the Wave Function," as
immortalized by Schrodinger with his
famous cat that is dead and alive at once
until some scoundrel opens the lid to its box.
Then you're dead period or alive
(probably some middle range option as well,
you know, like the living dead.)

Amazing stuff for sure . . . but why am I
always thinking of Dr. Frankenstein.
How about chain reactions? Is it possible

that the parallel might suck us all into it
and we'd take one final glance goodbye
and wind up in some shady realm
where someone offers you a phial of blood?
On the other hand, make that not Hades
but St. Croix and I'm all for it.
Where's the keyboard? Bring on the
daiquiris, silicon and suds, cocoanuts,
no snow or ice (ever!), sunshine,
equatorial breezes and ah! youth—
a parallel where the center always holds
and no old pensioner spits into the face of time
for the usual transfiguration.

Blank

Sometimes you must sit blankly before the blank screen
and wait, usually for nothing, and before that, the blank

sheet rolled into a typewriter or the fountain pen
clutched between your fingers before that same blank.

More likely it will emerge unexpectedly, the sudden
dart of a hummingbird across the blank of sky,

the firing of a neuron that yanks up from the blank depths
of memory that same hummingbird decades before

in the lush gardens of Miss Yunt in the corner house
on Columbus Street . . .

And this holds for just about everything you can name—
her eyes peering into your eyes as you turn randomly

in a library aisle, that musty old stone building, full
of germinated blanks, but her eyes, a new mystery,

a succession of blanks and the filling up of blanks and the
next emptying into new blanks, the blank before profusion,

before corruption, before annihilation and resurrection,
before the dove rains light into your empty vessel,

the blank you were before she said "I love you," before
temptation, before succumbing, before the long sprawl,

the blank you were before the explosion into birth,
the sliding in and out of nothing into something.

The interweaving, the dance, the duet, the moon
and the eclipse . . .

Faust Speaks

Time to set the record straight
now that infamy doesn't matter,
now that it's cool and chic
to embarrass yourself on Dr. Phil.
Look, no demons dragged me screaming
down to hell. Hell is a furnished room
with old dingy appliances
and a set of moldy Reader's Digest
condensed novels. And rats, of course.
No, I merely remained on my job
as an insurance agent—divorced,
eternal child support, no savings,
living off canned beans, no portfolio,
and an eight-year-old Dodge.

The Devil lied. I didn't get Shakira,
I acquired no knowledge, both of which
I craved. They sent a cheap floozy
with old fuzzy sailor tattoos, not the new
artwork on the skin of clean girls
I see on the streets, on campuses,
in Food Lion. Rank perfume shrouded
that broad and I nearly gagged to death.
No looker either, forty or so, overweight,
horse breath, a chain smoker . . .
but even she left me after a few months.
And she was my last shot.

As for knowledge, they sent a crate
of water-stained, dog-eared World Books
from Good Will, with instructions.
I had to read the damned things.

I refused of course. The desire
was instant omniscience without
working at it, without effort or pain.
That freak in the literature was not me
and I will testify in court on that point.
Not that it matters. Not that anyone cares.

I am old news, and old news now means
it didn't happen. I will say this for
Mephistopheles: pretty dapper for a con man,
a real seducer with his aquamarine bow tie,
glowing spats and those neon suspenders.
You just had to believe him.
My soul? Hell, I signed on the dotted line.
They took it all right and dropped it
into an old wooden cigar box, puny insect
it was. Why they craved it I don't know.
I don't miss the bitch at all.

Monstrosity

I passed a flatbed truck on I-81
a few hours ago, a truck that bore
on its flatness this monstrous
piece of, I assume, equipment.

The thing was massive and rusted
and flared out in all directions
with endless sprockets and gears
and springs, levers, turbines, bolts.

I wondered about its possible use,
no doubt industrial, maybe military . . .
it almost resembled the skeleton
of some ancient alien beast,

the sort of thing space travelers
encounter in the movies when they
move in to explore some erratic blips
on their oscilloscopes.

If women ruled the world, I thought,
no such behemoth would have been
constructed; or if we had remained
proto-human, the thing, sunken

in some bog, might be worshipped.
I glance over at the driver of the truck
as I passed. He wore a baseball cap
and a cigar butt dangled from his lip

as he thumped the dash with his free palm
to some music I could not hear.
Why do I presume country?

He seemed an ordinary enough fellow
hauling a cargo of pure evil
to a hive of clandestine saboteurs—
merely the delivery boy who, if questioned,
might snap *I don't know nothing.*

And at this moment I spin backward
in time to a cave in Cumae where
the sibyl, enshrouded in incense and smoke,
intones gibberish we once took as wisdom.

We now dismiss such muttering as superstition,
magic, primitive, worthless babble;
we deem the monstrosity as progress.
We flick on the lights and our houses glow.

Tropical Life

Szilard proved that the same equation
that governs entropy governs information theory.
Of course I don't get it, why should I?
But very interesting, strange bedfellows here.
Entropy, that demon of aging, decay and death
somehow throbs in the pulse of everyday data,
say, your receipt from Food Lion or the e-mail
you sent to Gloria or the grocery list taped
to your refrigerator. And we know too
that "information" relies upon noise and redundancy
which means that most of it belongs
with the garbage—and yet if it weren't for
that garbage what we know would glut our minds
and like Luria's mnemonist we could not function
given the avalanche of novelty we endure
each sunrise. So what ho? Why does any of this
pertain and how should we proceed?
Can we say that we should not proceed
since any procession means marching backward
to the usual fifes and bagpipes;
perhaps *what is* and *what is not* pertinent
were once inseparable, the Chang & Eng's
of holy matrimony.

    Ah, some kind soul
has just brought over a salver of dewy melons,
grapes, Assyrian figs and kumquats
from Louisiana. And the view here
is superb what with the sudsy waves carbonating
my toes, what with bikinied apparitions
boomeranging Frisbees in the distance
and codgers with their metal detectors
excavating the golden teeth of Jesus.

Ah, tropics! How you mandate the collapse
of theory and confusion and whatever
information we cram into old luggage
stuffed aboard the train to the nowhere
of everywhere.

Critical Theory

Remembrance is an act of defiance against time,
within time, of constructing a mythic self,
what you regard as you, whereas forgetting
is an act of deconstruction of that self in time,
and defiance by default. Who reads the text?
Who loves you? Hates you? Have you read
the tome that is you, have you explicated?
Are you a poem or a sprawling *Moby Dick*
of a novel? Or maybe a fiscal report, a spread sheet
of desire, a philosophic musing about musing?

Up by frail rung you go, out of the quagmire
of oblivion, memory, the sequential sequins,
most lost in the diaspora of exploration, a few
sticking onto the heart, the loins, the lips or brain—
you never know which or why.
You have lost most of yourself, the volume,
the oeuvre, always incomplete, the reader
perplexed over missing pages, words, images,
the reader also a text being read by you,
two readers, mislaid pages, signifieds without
signifiers . . . no wonder the conflict, the
declarations of war, the woe and beseeching . . .
and sometimes, magically, consummation

as if the missing pages, those leafy sequins,
tell the whole story, the ultimate Ur-legend,
and the incomplete text shrivels to dissemblance
and defect, and you, an imposter the Other surmises,
the Other equally masqueraded, duplicitous,

two prone haphazardly on a mattress neither owns
in a room far from home, though what is home
and where, when identity twists askew?
I asked the Philosopher to decipher me these deceits.
He (she?) said: play along, triumph assures defeat.
All plots lead to death, the echo in your dying breath.

Recruitment (With Bosco)

We're off visiting one college after another
in the Commonwealth so my youngest daughter
can decide for the Fall, and, right now,
a student tour guide leads us along varied walkways
of a rather dumpy campus (though some parts
are Jeffersonian impressive), and the guide
walks backward to face us, a rather morose
group of twelve or so parents and students,
bantering chipperly about this and that,
especially the diversity of the school
(one Jew, twelve blacks, two Hispanics) . . .

well, it's a small private place, muy expensive
I might add . . . and she brags about
the Olympic-sized pool and the fabulous
cafeteria food, yet none of us really want
to hear chit-chat, we just wanna see the place,
size up the lay of the land (just the facts, ma'am)
and it's stifling and sweltering, we're sweating,
thirsty, miserable, yes, we're a sorry group,
solemn, pissed off, sleepy, harried
(and we're ninety miles Tennessee-ward
from home), when suddenly, as if out of nowhere,
this pooch, a sort of battered Boston terrier,
trots briskly towards our group, a mutt aging along
with the rest of us, rather filthy and mottled,
and he's in the distance for the nonce,
but gaining, gaining on us, and it's his zealous
intent that amuses me, all business, as if
he's part of the group now, which he is,
and he trots along right beside me, tongue
flapping as he huffs, short stubby tail awag,

and he and I make eye contact, that's it,
we're partners now, he keeps looking at me,
and I return the gaze and start to laugh,
in fact, I can't stop laughing although I try
to stifle it as a cough but it's obvious I'm
laughing and the guide gives me the evil eye
since I imagine she thinks I'm laughing at her,
but no, the dog (whom I've named Bosco
because he's the color of that awful drink
my mother made me drink as a child)—

but it's not even Bosco I'm laughing at
though I suspect he's the fool Shakespeare missed,
making mock of our entire enterprise here
by imitating us! It's the situation,
we, a group on serious business involving lots of money,
and here's Bosco, jaunting along, for five buildings now,
sticking close to me, though he refuses to actually enter
any of the buildings, he merely waits for us to finish
and exit, and the guide has tried to give him the slip
by exiting on the rear side of where we are now,
the gymnasium, and I am dismayed that the ruse has worked–
but wait! here comes Bosco spinning round the corner
of the edifice, racing toward us, the guide
who has ignored Bosco all this time now shooting
venomous glances his way, and I lag behind the group
so Bosco can catch up, which he does, impervious,
cocky, all canine smiles as he glances adoringly
at me. But sad to say, we're back at the bursar's office
and must leave Bosco behind, which he senses,
for he takes one sniff, turns away, gives me
a last backward glance and ambles away . . . I see

another tour group across campus and he heads their way.
I like to think I made a friend this day, a goofy little creature
who, merely by existing, puts all of our grand enterprises
to shame. And on the drive home at sunset I start
to laugh again and my wife and girls laugh
and no doubt Bosco, still on campus, never stops laughing
as he sinks his teeth into the marrow
of that juicy bone we call wisdom.

Grasshopper While Reading Isaiah

for Billy Collins

and the inhabitants thereof are as grasshoppers
the Lord himself shall give you a sign

A day of calamity it was, misery
heaped upon woe, nothing extraordinary, no cataclysms,
just surfeit, accumulation: regrets, sorrows, grievances, shame . . .
all the stuff Americans aren't supposed to excavate,
the stuff Billy Collins doesn't want to write about
though, however boldly he labors,
his poems cannot really veil their shadows . . .
      make thy shadow as of night in the midst of the noonday
the stuff Unamuno and Portuguese fishermen
and the crafty, sultry Greeks sipping ouzo in cafes
take for granted, which makes me suspect
I'm not American but some throwback to the Salerno
of my great-grandfather, or deeper, an Armenian woman
shrouded in black beating her chest in the holiest niche
of a stone church . . .
      Then said I, woe is me! for I am undone
well, anyway, I go to bed early after a cup or two
of Pinot Noir and some Benadryl (I really want to sleep
this time, not writhe) and know the potions will take effect
in about half an hour, and thus can read a few more chapters
of Isaiah the prophet (I'm up to Hezekiah weeping sorely
after Isaiah tells him, via of course God, that he will perish
      In those days was Hezekiah sick unto death
yet the Lord spared him, added fifteen more years
to his life as *a nail in a sure place*) . . .
and what fantastic poetry it is, no Billy Collins dumping
on despair and angst, but true majestic terrors and horror

everyone shall howl, weeping abundantly
and as I glide into bed I notice the greenest grasshopper,
greener than green, and *at an instant suddenly,*
alighted on the adjacent pillow, a big one too, fat with life
　　　my leanness, my leanness, woe unto me!
and voltage, green and sculpted, and I swear gazing at me,
so I put Isaiah down to return the favor
(how often does a grasshopper visit your bed?)
and, well, maybe Billy's right after all,
for, as the internet informs us, grasshoppers are totems
of prosperity; and the Japanese believe that the moon
solicits their song; and the wise Chinese with their fortune cookies
and cadmium regard it as a symbol of longevity, happiness
(happiness!), fertility, and a lot more; and the Iroquois
proclaim it gospel, a harbinger of glad tidings,
and since it remains mostly on the ground, a token of stability
and security . . . and on it goes . . . and I, seeker of omens,
cherish this visit from an alien species and wish I could
drag it out, probe it, cultivate it, but the grasshopper soon
turns its back on me and flits off somewhere
(I pray this does not reverse the magic)
and by this point I'm too zonked to seek it out,
scoop and drop into a bush outside, so I resume Isaiah . . .
　　　and when they arose early in the morning,
　　　behold, they were all dead corpses
and the carnage and apocalypse continueth apace
and I'm fastly drifting into the reverie Billy talks about,
musing over time and space and the years leapfrogging
into . . . what? and I yearn for *the city of confusion*
to be *broken down* as does Billy in that poem
about deathbeds, a final moment of rigid clarity,
but yet the fear

I am deprived of the residue of my years
that at an instant sudden the poet's millennium
will crumble and he will request one final dance
with the beloved, his hand secured delicately
on the small of her back as Isaiah rages on the mountain
denouncing iniquity and false idols,
　　arising to shake terribly the earth,
and I forsake both Billy and the prophet,
sweep off the covers and prowl the room
in search of that grasshopper,
my speech whispering from the dust *woe,*
because still other sources deem them
augers of pestilence, devastation and death.

About the Author

Two volumes of Louis Gallo's poetry, *Crash* and *Clearing the Attic,* will be published by Adelaide. A third, *Archaeology,* has been published by Kelsay Books; Kelsay will also publish a fourth volume, *Scherzo Furiant.* Gallo's work has appeared or will shortly appear in *Wide Awake in the Pelican State* (LSU anthology), *Southern Literary Review, Fiction Fix, Glimmer Train, Hollins Critic, Rattle, Southern Quarterly, Litro, New Orleans Review, Xavier Review, Glass: A Journal of Poetry, Missouri Review, Mississippi Review, Texas Review, Baltimore Review, Pennsylvania Literary Journal, The Ledge, storySouth, Houston Literary Review, Tampa Review, Raving Dove, The Journal (Ohio), Greensboro Review,* and many others. His chapbooks include *The Truth Changes, The Abomination of Fascination, Status Updates and The Ten Most Important Questions.* Louis is the founding editor of the now-defunct journals, *The Barataria Review* and *Books: A New Orleans Review.* His work has been nominated for the Pushcart Prize several times. He is the recipient of an NEA grant for fiction. He teaches at Radford University in Radford, Virginia.